LIVING WITH THE SENECAS

A Creative Minds Biography

LIVING WITH THE SENECAS

A Story about Mary Jemison

by Susan Bivin Aller

illustrations by Laurie Harden

M Millbrook Press/Minneapolis

For the Wednesday Writers —SBA

In dedication to my mother, Patricia S. Harden, who taught me to draw and instilled in me the love of art. And to all my models, who have served for the sake of art, willingly or unwillingly, valiantly, and with great humor. —LH

Text copyright © 2007 by Susan Bivin Aller
Illustrations copyright © 2007 by Millbrook Press, Inc.

Map on pp. 58–59 by Laura Westlund

Millbrook Press, Inc.
A division of Lerner Publishing Group
241 First Avenue North
Minneapolis, MN 55401 U.S.A.

Website address: www.lernerbooks.com

Library of Congress Cataloging-in-Publication Data

Aller, Susan Bivin.
    Living with the Senecas : a story about Mary Jemison / by Susan
Bivin Aller ; illustrated by Laurie Harden.
        p. cm. — (Creative minds biographies)
    Includes bibliographical references and index.
    ISBN-13: 978–0–8225–5989–4 (lib. bdg. : alk. paper)
    ISBN-10: 0–8225–5989–7 (lib. bdg. : alk. paper)
    1. Jemison, Mary, 1743–1833—Juvenile literature. 2. Pioneers—
Genesee River Valley (Pa. and N.Y.)—Biography—Juvenile literature.
3. Indian captivities—Genesee River Valley (Pa. and N.Y.)—Juvenile
literature. 4. Genesee River Valley (Pa. and N.Y.)—Biography—
Juvenile literature. I. Harden, Laurie, ill. II. Title. III. Series: Creative
minds biography.
E99.S3J4563 2007
974.7'8803092—dc22
    [B]   2006016785

Manufactured in the United States of America
1 2 3 4 5 6 – JR – 12 11 10 09 08 07

Table of Contents

1

Captured!

Mary Jemison hurried as fast as she could through the darkening woods. She had only a few yards to go before the trees ended. Then she would be in the neighbors' field and within sight of their log house.

Father wanted to borrow the neighbors' horse so he could finish spring plowing tomorrow. Even though the sun was almost down, Father had told fifteen-year-old Mary to go for the horse this evening. She could stay overnight with the neighbors and bring the horse back early in the morning. Mary wasn't exactly scared. But she knew American Indians had been raiding nearby Pennsylvania settlements.

Thomas and Jane Jemison—Father and Mother—worried for their family's safety. They had worked hard since they came to America from Ireland in 1743. Mary was born at sea on the ship carrying her parents, two brothers, and a sister. Now there were two more brothers, born in America. The family owned its own land. Father said he wasn't going to be scared off by talk of Indians. He would stay on his land.

Suddenly, Mary stopped in her tracks, her heart pounding. She sensed that something was coming toward her. It was not on the path but floating silently from the sky. She saw a great sheet close around her, and then everything went black.

When Mary woke up, she found herself in a bed in the neighbors' house. Her neighbors hovered near her, giving thanks when Mary opened her eyes. They told her they had found her lying on the path near their house and that she had been unconscious all night. What had happened to her?

She told them about seeing a mysterious sheet floating toward her and the feeling that she had been caught up in it. Was this strange vision a warning? Was she or her family in danger?

Filled with worry, Mary returned home with the borrowed horse early in the morning. She was relieved to see that life was going on as usual.

Mother was preparing breakfast for the family and some visiting neighbors. Father was outside near the house, making an ax handle, and Mary's two older brothers were working in the barn.

As they were sitting down for breakfast, a horse galloped up and they heard gunshots. The women pulled their children to them. Cautiously, they opened the door. There on the ground lay a neighbor and his horse, both shot dead.

At once, several Shawnee Indians crowded into the house and herded the women and children out into the yard. At the same time, other Shawnees grabbed Mary's father and tied his hands behind his back. Somehow, Mary's two older brothers managed to escape from the barn. Mary didn't see them again.

The Shawnee men grabbed all the food they could carry. Then they forced their prisoners to move quickly away from the house and into the woods. Mary saw that four of their captors were white men wearing the uniform of the French army. She had heard that the French and Shawnees were working together to push the English and Irish settlers off the land. So it was true, then.

Mary stumbled along, helping the younger children keep up. The Shawnee in the rear whipped them when they dragged behind.

The terrible journey lasted all day. The Shawnees didn't let the terrified group pause even once to rest or eat. They made the smaller children drink urine when they cried for water. Mary and the adults took turns carrying the little ones when they fell exhausted.

When night came, the captors made their prisoners lie on the ground, without any shelter or a fire to keep them warm. Mary knew that her older brothers had escaped. She expected them to bring others from the settlement to save them. So did the Shawnees. That was why they were in such a hurry to move deep into the woods and not leave any sign of where they were heading. The Shawnees guarded the captives closely all night, in case anyone tried to escape.

The group was made to get up before dawn. They walked and walked. Mary and the others were close to collapse when they were finally allowed to stop. The Shawnees set out bread and meat they had taken from the Jemisons' house. Mary's mother urged her children to eat to keep up their strength for whatever lay ahead. But Mary's father was in such a state of shock that he couldn't eat a bite. Mary saw that he had given up all hope of rescue.

The forced march continued for a second day. About noon they passed a small fort, and Mary heard her father say its name—Fort Canagojigge.

These were the only words she heard him utter the whole time. Mary desperately hoped someone in the fort would see them and come to save them. But there was no one. The fort seemed to be abandoned.

Near dusk, Mary saw that they had reached the edge of a swamp surrounded by small hemlock trees and tangled bushes. Hidden in this dank place, the Shawnees stopped and made camp for the night. Again, the captives ate meat and bread taken from the Jemisons' home. Their spirits were so low that food did little to help.

After supper, a Shawnee replaced Mary's worn, dirty shoes and stockings with a pair of clean new moccasins. Then he did the same to one of the little neighbor boys who had been visiting the Jemison house. Instead of being glad for the comfort of the soft moccasins, Mary felt a new terror. She realized this simple act meant that she and the boy were being prepared to continue traveling with the Shawnee Indians. None of the other captives, including her family, was given moccasins. Would the others be left behind? Or even killed?

Mary's mother had the same fears. She drew her daughter aside and put her arm around her. "My dear little Mary," she said, "I fear that the time has arrived when we must be parted forever. Your life . . . I think will be spared. . . . Remember my child your own name, and the name of your father and mother. Be careful and do not forget your English tongue. . . . Don't try to escape; for if you do they will find and destroy you."

Weeping and clinging to each other, Mary and her family were separated by the Shawnees. As she was led away with the little boy to a distant part of the swamp, she heard her mother calling after her, "Don't cry, Mary, don't cry my child. God will bless you. Farewell, farewell."

Nightmare

One of the Shawnee Indians forced Mary and the boy to lie down in a sheltered spot. The little boy begged Mary to run away, but Mary remembered her mother's last words. "If you try to escape, they will find and destroy you."

As Mary lay shivering in the cold night, she thought about her family and their happy life. What would become of her now?

In her first few years on the Pennsylvania frontier, Mary's only fears were for the safety of their cattle and sheep. Wild animals, such as wolves and panthers, sometimes entered their settlement and stole livestock for dinner.

Mary's family had moved from Philadelphia to their home on Marsh Creek, near what became Gettysburg. At Marsh Creek, Father built a log house and a barn. He carved fields in the rich soil. Every year he planted crops, and every year he grew more prosperous. Three years ago, however, Mary and her family had begun to hear horrifying stories of American Indians raiding white settlements.

A war was raging over the control of Native American lands in Ohio, Pennsylvania, and New York. People called the war the French and Indian War because American Indians and French worked together to raid British settlements and forts. By 1757 so many white people had been killed or burned out by American Indians and French soldiers that an army was formed to protect the settlements. A young colonel named George Washington was one of the army's commanders.

The army was a long way from the Jemisons' farm at Marsh Creek, however. Some of the Jemisons' neighbors had already gone back to the safety of Philadelphia, but Father thought he could fight off any attackers. Now, as she shivered in fear, Mary knew it was too late for anybody to save them.

Early the next morning, the other Shawnees and the French soldiers came to where Mary and the boy were still closely guarded. There was no sign of her family or the boy's family. Mary wept. She was sure that Mother and Father, her sister and brothers, and the neighbor woman with her children must have been killed during the night.

On this third day of captivity, the group moved more quickly because there were fewer of them. One Shawnee Indian followed behind, sweeping the grass and weeds with a stick to erase signs of their footprints. It grew colder and began to rain. Mary and the others struggled on. That night the Shawnees gathered wood for a fire and made a shelter of branches. It was the only comfort in a night that was becoming a nightmare.

After eating, some of the Shawnees opened their bags and pulled out fresh, bloody scalps. They stretched the scalps over small hoops to dry by the fire. Then they scraped, combed, and painted them. Mary nearly fainted. She recognized the scalps with her mother's red hair and her father's and the children's.

The Shawnees tried to explain to Mary that they had not wanted to kill her family. But a small group could move more quickly than a large group.

Mary was sure that her older brothers and neighbors had been close to finding them. But if the bodies of her family had been left behind, the neighbors would assume they were all dead. Mary could not escape and had no hope of being rescued.

The next day's journey took Mary and her captors higher into the Allegheny Mountains. The weather grew freezing cold, and the steady rain turned to heavy spring snow. For three nights, the group stayed in a shelter made of branches. Mary and the little boy huddled together for warmth and comfort.

On the seventh day, a group of six more Native Americans joined them. They had captured a white boy about her age. Mary hoped he might help her escape, but he was so exhausted that he was barely able to move. That night the captors roasted a deer for supper.

At last, on the eighth day, the group arrived at Fort Duquesne on the Ohio River, near where modern-day Pittsburgh stands. French soldiers and American Indians occupied the fort. Before entering the fort, the Shawnees combed Mary's and the boys' hair and painted it bright red.

The men took Mary and the boys to a small house inside the fort and locked them in. They were left alone all night. They lay awake, imagining all kinds of terrible things that might happen to them. Would they be killed with a tomahawk like their families had been? Or burned alive, as Mary had heard sometimes happened? Or would they be set free in the forest, only to be gobbled up by wild beasts?

When morning came at last, the captives were let out of the house. The two boys were taken away by some Frenchmen. Mary never saw the boys again nor found out what happened to them.

Mary was alive, but she was all alone in a strange and frightening world. Just then, two women of another tribe—the Seneca—entered the fort and began to look Mary over. They talked to the Shawnees who had captured Mary. Mary was made to understand that the Shawnees were giving her to the Seneca women. Mary was somewhat relieved to see that the women had pleasant faces and treated her kindly.

The two Senecas took Mary in a canoe down the Ohio River toward their home near present-day Steubenville, Ohio. In front of them, the Shawnees traveled in a larger canoe. Mary hid her face from the awful sight of her family's scalps strung from a pole in the Shawnees' canoe.

When the Seneca women reached their town at the mouth of the Shenanjee River, they took off Mary's filthy, tattered clothes and threw them into the river.

Then they bathed her and dressed her in fresh new Seneca garments. They sat her down in the middle of a large room in their bark-covered wigwam. A few minutes later, all the women of the town crowded around her and immediately began a chorus of wailing and crying. A leader began a long speech that was half talking, half singing.

The women were obviously very upset about something that had happened. Mary was somehow at the center of their attention. But why? What was to be her fate?

Adopted

Mary sat perfectly still, hardly daring to breathe, as the singing and chanting continued. The women followed the leader's movements and emotions. They were mourning the death of a young warrior in battle. He was the brother of the two Seneca women who brought Mary to their home. Mary had been given to the Seneca women as a replacement for their brother. It was a Seneca custom to give a captive to a family who had lost a loved one.

As the long ceremony came to an end, Mary felt the mood change. The women began to smile at her and spoke to her in kind voices. She understood that she was being welcomed into the tribe. This adoption ceremony ended when she was given a Seneca name: De-he-wa-mis. Mary's name meant "Two Falling Voices." From that moment on, Mary was treated as a full sister by the women to whom she had been given.

In less than two weeks, Mary's life had been turned upside down. Her family members had died terrible deaths. She had traveled far from home and was living with American Indians, whom she had always feared and hated. But her two Seneca sisters treated Mary gently and with sympathy. Mary knew that they also understood what it was like to lose loved ones.

The sisters did not want Mary to speak English when she was with them but taught her their language, which she learned easily. However, Mary repeated prayers in English whenever she was alone, to obey her mother's last request to always remember her English tongue.

Mary was expected to work along with the other women. She took care of the younger children and did housework. Great sadness and loneliness nearly overcame her, but her Seneca family tried to comfort her. Mary had arrived at the village when it was time for spring planting, so she went with the other women and children to the fields.

In Seneca life, planting was the work of women, not of men as it had been in the white world. While women worked in the fields, the Seneca men went hunting and fishing and brought home game and fish.

The Senecas' spring planting seemed easier and more pleasant than the way her father had done it. He had worked alone, walking behind a team of oxen hitched to a plow. The Seneca women, on the other hand, all worked together in one field. They made light work of planting by using short-handled hoes to dig holes. Then they sowed the beans, squash, or corn. As they worked, they talked and laughed and let their children play nearby.

The tribe celebrated the planting and growing seasons with ceremonial dances and songs. They praised the Great Spirit and asked for good harvests. They honored the women who grew the crops that fed the people.

Spring turned to summer. Mary helped tend the crops and learned to pound corn, roast deer meat, and bake corn cakes in the ashes. Although she grieved for her family, Mary was warmed by the kindness and affection of her new Seneca family. She had seen them act cruelly when they wanted revenge or justice. But she also saw how peacefully they lived with their friends and families and how fair they were in all their dealings.

"My situation was easy; I had no particular hardships to endure," Mary recalled later. "[My sisters] were kind good natured women; . . . decent in their habits, and very tender and gentle towards me."

After the harvest, it was time for the tribe to move to their winter camp. Women were in charge of all the packing and moving. It didn't take them long to get ready. Each family had deerskin beds and platters and bowls made of bark. They also had iron kettles, tin cups, and utensils from their trading with the French and British. Mary helped the women load these things and the grain into large canoes and onto horses. Then the families left behind their empty, bark-covered wigwams. They began the yearly trip to their hunting grounds at the mouth of the Scioto River near present-day Portsmouth, Ohio.

During the winter months, the men hunted for meat, skins, and furs. There were many deer and elk in the forest. Smaller animals such as beaver and muskrat lived in the marshes near the river.

It was the work of women to bring the freshly killed game into camp and prepare it. Mary, who had turned sixteen, learned to preserve meat for food. She cleaned the fur pelts that would be traded for white men's goods. She helped prepare deerskin to make moccasins and clothing.

Mary's birth mother had taught her how to spin thread and to knit and weave cloth. From the Senecas, she was learning how to make clothing and other household items from soft deerskin. They sewed the pieces together with animal sinew, or tendons.

In spring when ice melted on the rivers and travel by canoe was possible, Mary and the tribe went back to their town on the Shenanjee River. For the second time, Mary helped with the spring planting. Later, the entire tribe, including Mary, traveled to Fort Duquesne to trade skins and furs with the fort's new British owners. The British had captured Fort Duquesne from the French and renamed it Fort Pitt.

The Senecas made camp on the shore of the river across from the fort. For the first time since her early days of captivity, Mary saw white people and heard them speaking English. She later said her heart "bounded to be liberated from the Indians and to be restored to my friends and my country."

When she and the Senecas crossed the river in their canoes and landed at the fort, the people there were astonished to see a young, fair-haired woman in Seneca dress. Mary was small for her age and appeared frail in comparison to the strong, athletic American Indians. The British were curious. How did she come to be living with the Senecas? What was her name? Where and when was she captured?

Mary eagerly told them her story, and she became more and more excited as she realized that she might be able to escape. She had adjusted well to Seneca ways and was fond of her Seneca sisters. Yet when she heard white men speaking English, her only thought was to return to the world of her birth.

Mary's Seneca sisters didn't want her to talk to the British. The British might try to keep her at the fort. Quickly, the sisters pulled Mary into their canoe and rowed back across the river to their camp. They hurriedly packed their belongings into the canoe—even taking their half-baked bread from the fire. They took off down the river with Mary between them in the canoe. They kept rowing all the way to their hometown, where they could keep Mary safe.

Mary learned afterward that the British did, indeed, come for her almost immediately after she left with her sisters. The white men searched the camp, certain that Mary was hidden somewhere. But they were too late. Mary once again had been taken captive.

Belonging

This near rescue threw Mary into a depression again. She worked as always, but she felt the same hopelessness she had felt after her first captivity. This time she recovered more quickly. She and her Seneca family had become very fond of one another in the year they had been together. Mary not only had two Seneca sisters but she also had Seneca brothers and their wives and children. Gradually, her gloom lifted.

In the following year, Mary's tribe built a new town about twenty miles north of present-day Huntington, West Virginia. They called it Wiishto. One day Mary's Seneca sisters told her they had arranged for her to marry a Delaware Indian who was visiting her tribe. Seventeen-year-old Mary didn't want to get married, but she had no choice. The man's name was Sheninjee. He was a large and handsome man, generous and well respected by the other Native Americans.

Mary soon discovered that he was also very kind and tender toward her. They were married, and it wasn't long before she truly fell in love with him. In the second summer at Wiishto, Mary gave birth to a daughter, who lived only two days. Two years later, Mary had a healthy baby boy. She named him Thomas Jemison after her father.

By this time, Mary was so accustomed to life with the Senecas that she had almost forgotten her wish to return to the white world. Only occasionally did she think about her beloved parents and the home in Pennsylvania. The American Indian world had become her world. "With them was my home," she said. "My family was there, and there I had many friends to whom I was warmly attached."

When her baby Thomas was about four months old, Mary and Sheninjee began a long journey on the Ohio

River. They were going north to visit Mary's two Seneca sisters. The women had moved with other family members to a Seneca town on the Genesee River not far from present-day Rochester, New York. Mary's two Seneca brothers traveled with Mary and her husband. They piled furs and skins into a large canoe to trade at Fort Pitt for white men's goods. On the way, they passed a British trading post and were surprised that no one was there. Shortly afterward, they saw the bodies of three traders from the post floating in the river.

Sheninjee quickly turned the canoe and went back to the trading post, fearing that white men would be searching the river for the traders' murderers. At the post, they found a raiding party of Shawnees. Shawnees and Senecas were friends, so there was no reason to be afraid of them. The Shawnees were torturing a young white man. The sight of his blood and pain brought back such horrors that Mary cried out for the Shawnees to release him. Finally, they did let him go, and he ran off, bleeding, into the woods and disappeared.

Later, Mary, Thomas, Sheninjee, and her Seneca brothers continued their journey on the river. Along the way, they stayed for short periods with other Indian bands. Summer was nearly over when another of Mary's Seneca brothers arrived at the town where they were staying. This brother lived with the part of his tribe that made their home on the Genesee River. Each year he traveled between that family and Mary's. He told Mary that her sisters missed her very much and longed to see her and her baby. Sheninjee agreed to let Mary and the baby go to the Genesee with her brothers. But he decided to spend the winter in the south to hunt game. He told Mary he would come to the Genesee to bring her back in the spring.

Mary's trip from Ohio to New York took place in 1762. It was a dangerous time to travel. The French and Indian War was spreading throughout Ohio, Pennsylvania, and New York. Mary had experienced the war firsthand when her family was captured in Pennsylvania four years earlier. She was in danger again, but this time as a member of an American Indian tribe, not as a white settler.

Mary and her three Seneca brothers left the river and started overland on foot. Mary carried her baby, who was then about nine months old, on her back. The men knew how to find their way, but to Mary it looked like a wilderness without end. Day after day they walked, Mary carrying her heavy son and struggling to keep up. She had only a blanket as a wrap. This protected her from rain and cold and became her bed on the hard ground at night.

One day they came to a town of the Delaware Indians. No one was there. Mary's brothers knew that American Indians usually hid food when they left a town, in case they ever returned. So the men searched and found a large supply of dried corn, beans, sugar, and honey. The discovery was a great stroke of luck. They had not been carrying much food with them, and they still had a long way to go. They also found several horses, and that made their travel easier.

Autumn arrived. Cold rains began to fall, and Mary was constantly chilled through. She protected her baby as well as she could, but her blanket was wet and her horse slipped over rocky ground and through mud. Once the group had to wait several days to cross a creek swollen by rains. Finally, they mounted their horses and made them swim across. Mary and her baby came close to drowning.

At long last, they reached their destination, Little Beard's Town on the Genesee River. They had traveled nearly 700 miles—236 by canoe, 175 by foot, and 270 with horses!

Mary's two sisters ran to meet her. They took her to their mother, who received her as joyfully as if she were her own daughter. Mary's family made room in their longhouse for her and her baby. A central fire heated the house and served as a stove for cooking.

Thick furs on low platforms around the sides of the room made snug beds.

"The warmth of their feelings, and the continued favors that I received at their hands," said Mary, "riveted my affection for them so strongly that I [believe] I loved them as I should have loved my own sister had she lived."

5

Landowner

For hundreds of years, the land and waterways along the Genesee River had been home to the Iroquois Indians. There were five Iroquois-speaking nations: the Senecas, the Oneidas, the Onondagas, the Mohawks, and the Cayugas. Their people were united in a federation. By 1722, a sixth group, the Tuscaroras, had joined the federation. Together the Iroquois occupied lands all along the Great Lakes of Erie and Ontario and south into Pennsylvania and Ohio. The Genesee River area was especially precious to the Senecas. They believed the beautiful river valley, with its deep gorges and rushing waterfalls, was home to their sacred spirits.

Little Beard's Town, where Mary and her family lived, was the largest of several towns in the region. It was made up of more than one hundred pole and bark longhouses. Seneca life centered on women, who owned the longhouses. Women were in charge of all household affairs and the planting and harvesting of crops. Women arranged marriages. When a couple married, they moved in with the wife's mother and sisters, and the family's longhouse was made larger. Property passed from mother to daughter instead of from father to son (the custom in most white societies). Spiritual leaders were often women, and women even had the power to declare war and to decide the fate of prisoners of war.

Mary arrived in late 1762, as the men in Little Beard's Town were preparing to do battle against the British at Fort Erie. She watched the men paint their bodies and gather their weapons. Then they marched off to join their French allies in a raid on the fort. When the men returned victorious a few days later, they brought with them two white prisoners. A day of celebration followed. Mary's sisters urged her to go with them to the entertainment, or "frolic," as they called it. The Senecas were going to take revenge on the prisoners by torturing and executing them.

Mary's Seneca mother scolded her daughters. "How can you even think of attending the feast and seeing the unspeakable torments those poor unfortunate prisoners must inevitably suffer?" she asked. "And how can you think of conducting . . . your poor sister, who has so lately been a prisoner, who has lost her parents, [sister,] and brothers by the hands of bloody warriors?" Then she concluded, "Our task is quite easy at home, and our business needs our attention."

All winter Mary took part in the life of the large family that was her own. Her baby Thomas grew to be a sturdy one-year-old. Mary waited eagerly for spring and the return of her husband. As the weeks passed, however, she became more and more worried when Sheninjee did not arrive. It wasn't until summer that Mary heard news of him. Tragically, he had become ill soon after he and Mary parted and had died at Wiishto in the winter. Sheninjee may have died of smallpox, which raged through Delaware and Shawnee Indian towns in Ohio that year. Smallpox was spread by the British, who gave American Indians infected blankets that had been used by smallpox victims at Fort Pitt. Mary grieved for her beloved husband.

Although Mary felt at home in her Seneca tribe, the outside world of white people still considered her to be a captive of the Native Americans. Three years after Mary went to live at Little Beard's Town, Great Britain offered a reward to anyone who could save a white captive or prisoner of war. A greedy Seneca chief tried to force Mary to go with him to the nearest fort so he could collect reward money. One of Mary's Seneca brothers told the chief that he would kill Mary before he would let her be taken. Mary was faced with losing her family or her life.

Once again, her sisters saved her. They sent her to hide in a secret place far away from the house. When the chief was gone, they would send for her. Mary took the most precious thing in her life—her son, Thomas—and carried him through the night to safety. When the chief came to the longhouse to look for her, the sisters pretended not to know where she was. Finally, the chief gave up, and Mary's brother brought her and Thomas home.

This event made Mary's sisters decide to find her another husband to protect her. So they arranged another marriage for her. This time it was to an important Seneca warrior named Hiokatoo. Hiokatoo was unusually tall and strong and had a long record of bravery in war. He was often away fighting, even though he was considered old—in his fifties. He was more than thirty years older than Mary, but he became a kind and gentle husband, and she loved him.

In 1775 the American Revolution began between the British and the American colonists. Both the British and the Americans wanted the help of American Indian nations. The Senecas and the Mohawks agreed to fight alongside the British, against the Colonial American forces. Mary found herself involved in the war, not as a white American but as a Seneca Indian woman acting out of loyalty to her tribe. Her house in Little Beard's Town became a favorite stopover for the Mohawk leader Joseph Brant and his fellow officers. Mary gave them supplies and a change of clothing. And she fed them, sometimes working all night to make food for them.

Mary's town seemed far enough away from the major battles of the war to be safe. But the Native American and British attacks on frontier settlements in New York and Pennsylvania, led by Joseph Brant, finally angered the Americans enough to strike back. General George Washington recruited an army of four thousand men, led by General John Sullivan. Washington sent them to do battle with Brant's Mohawk and Seneca warriors and the British troops fighting with them. As the army approached Little Beard's Town, Mary and the other women took their children and fled to the woods for safety. By that time, Mary had five children, Thomas and four younger ones by her marriage with Hiokatoo.

General Sullivan's army destroyed Little Beard's Town and more than forty other towns. The soldiers burned ripe cornfields and threw stores of food into the river. They killed all the animals and chopped down the orchards. When Mary and the others dared to return, they found that all 128 houses had been burned. "There was not a mouthful of any kind of sustenance [food] left, not even enough to keep a child one day from perishing with hunger," Mary later recalled.

It was late autumn. Mary made a brave and desperate decision. "I immediately resolved to take my children and look out for myself, without delay." She traveled up the river a few miles to a piece of rich land called the Gardeau Flats. There she found a large field of corn waiting to be harvested. Two black men who had escaped from slavery in the South had planted it. They hired Mary to help harvest the corn. For her work, she received enough corn to feed her family. Mary said she laughed to herself when one of the men guarded her with a loaded gun so Indians wouldn't take her while she worked in the field. He didn't know that the nearby American Indians were her own tribe of Senecas and that she was perfectly safe.

That winter was the worst one Mary could remember. Many of Mary's tribe froze or starved to death. Deer and other animals also died in the extreme cold.

Mary, however, was fortunate. She and her children survived the winter in the cabin of the two men.

When spring came, Mary decided to build a cabin of her own and stay on the Gardeau Flats. Two years later, the men she worked for moved on to another place, leaving Mary and her family alone on the flats. Her husband was often absent, but Mary—like all Seneca women—knew how to plant and harvest. With her rich land along the river, she managed to survive better than most of her friends, whose fields, orchards, and livestock had been destroyed by the war.

The American Revolution ended in 1783. The United States won its independence from the British. The next year, the Iroquois Nations sold most of their lands in western New York, Pennsylvania, Ohio, and Kentucky to the United States. At the same time, the Americans offered Mary a chance to return to the white world. If she did, she would be treated as a full citizen of the United States of America.

Mary's eldest son, Thomas, was a young man of twenty-two. If Mary wanted to go back to the white world, she would need his help in guiding and protecting her and the younger children on their way back to her childhood home in Pennsylvania. The Seneca chiefs might have let Mary leave the tribe, but they refused to let Thomas go. He was too good a warrior.

And there was another issue that worried Mary: "I had got a large family of Indian children, that I must take with me," she said. "If I should be so fortunate as to find my (white) relatives, they would despise them, if not myself; and treat us as enemies, . . . which I thought I could not endure." Mary had heard that when her two older Jemison brothers escaped from the attack on their family, they had gone to live with their grandfather in Virginia. But they had not been in touch with Mary.

Mary finally decided. "It [is] my choice to stay and spend the remainder of my days with my Indian friends." Her Seneca family, she said, were "well pleased" with her decision.

At the Treaty of Big Tree in 1797, the Iroquois sold nearly all the rest of their lands west of the Genesee River to the United States. Mary's Seneca brother had asked the Iroquois council of chiefs to let Mary keep the Gardeau Flats, where she was living. The chiefs agreed. When the New York legislature made Mary a naturalized citizen twenty years later, they confirmed her title to own the land permanently.

Mary's huge piece of fertile farmland was about six miles wide and five miles long, with the Genesee River running through the middle of it.

As the years passed, the Gardeau Flats became sandwiched between the shrinking Seneca lands on the west and the rapidly approaching white settlements on the east. But the land was still Mary's. Her husband, Hiokatoo, died there in 1811 at the age of 103. Her daughters married and lived near her with their growing families. "For provisions I have never suffered since I came upon the flats," Mary said. "Nor have I ever been in debt to any other hands than my own for the plenty that I have shared."

White Woman of
the Genesee

To her Seneca and white neighbors, Mary became
known as the White Woman of the Genesee. Only a
few people knew the whole story of her long life,
however. Here was a woman born to an Irish
immigrant family who had, in the end, become De-
he-wa-mis, a loyal Seneca Indian by adoption. How
she survived captivity, wars, and hardships was both
interesting and historically important. Could someone interview her and write down her words? Dr.
James Seaver, who was a physician and an amateur
historian, said he would do it.

Mary toiled up the steep path toward the cabin where Dr. Seaver waited. The year was 1823. She walked steadily for a woman of eighty years, only occasionally holding onto the arm of the young neighbor who accompanied her. She wore typical Seneca clothing: a short brown flannel dress over cotton underclothing, all tied with deerskin strings. Around her legs she had wrapped and tied blue leggings. Buckskin moccasins covered her feet. Over her gray hair she wore a brown cloth cap tied like a sunbonnet.

Mary stopped to catch her breath. She had walked paths like this many times, sometimes carrying a baby strapped to her back, other times hauling boards to build a house or heavy bags of corn. She still worked hard every day. She fed her cows and chickens, harvested her crops, and cooked her meals. She even chopped her own wood.

Dr. Seaver met her at the door of the cabin. Mary greeted him in English, with the slight Irish accent that she still had. She lowered her head when she spoke to him and looked at him from under her eyebrows, as her American Indian friends usually did. Her blue eyes sparkled when she talked and frequently filled with tears as she told him the moving story of her life.

Mary spent three days being interviewed by Dr. Seaver. She told him about her early childhood in Pennsylvania with her Irish American family. And she told him about her Seneca family. "I have been the mother of eight children; three of whom are now living," she said proudly. "And I have at this time thirty-nine grandchildren and fourteen great-grandchildren." She was especially fond of one of her grandsons, who had graduated from Dartmouth College and was studying to become a doctor.

Not all the years had been good ones for Mary or her family, however. "[I] can truly say from my own experience," she told Seaver, "that the time at which parents take the most satisfaction and comfort with their families is when their children are young."

She had good reason to say this. By the time her sons grew up, they had become victims of white men's liquor—"poison," Mary called it. Her son John killed his older brother Thomas in a drunken rage in 1811. The next year, John and his youngest brother Jesse fought while drunk, and John killed him too. Five years later, John himself was murdered by drunken friends during a brawl. "[It was] enough to bring down my gray hairs with sorrow to the grave," Mary told Seaver, with tears welling in her eyes.

Not only did her sons cause her grief but dishonest white people took advantage of her and cheated her out of parts of her land. One day a man who said his name was George Jemison showed up at Mary's door, pretending to be a long-lost cousin of her father. Mary invited him to stay, since he had no money, and she ended up supporting him for some time. Meanwhile, he gained her trust more and more. Finally, he talked Mary into signing a paper giving him some of the Gardeau Flats. Mary ended up giving him four hundred acres, instead of the forty she had agreed to.

Four years after her interview with Dr. Seaver, Mary lost even more of her land through dealings with dishonest white people. All that remained to her were about two acres along the Genesee River, where Mary lived with her daughter Polly. Her other daughters and their families lived nearby. The Senecas sold the rest of their tribal land to white settlers. They moved away from the Genesee River to live on reservations, and Mary's family became an isolated Seneca community surrounded by white settlements. Mary's family missed their Seneca friends and families. So in 1831, Mary sold her land too and moved with her children and grandchildren to the Buffalo Creek Reservation. She wanted to spend her final days in the company of her chosen Seneca people.

Afterword

If Mary Jemison were interviewed in modern times, she would likely be filmed or recorded telling her story. When Dr. Seaver interviewed Mary Jemison in 1823, however, he had to take down what she said by hand. From his notes, he wrote a fascinating book about Mary Jemison's life. Those notes are lost. So it is impossible to know how much of the story is Mary's and how much is Dr. Seaver's interpretation. Dr. Seaver was not an experienced historian or journalist. He had probably read other stories of white people who were captured by American Indians. These stories were very popular at that time and may have influenced how Dr. Seaver reported Mary's words. When we read the story he wrote, we have to remember that we are listening to Mary's words as written and perhaps changed by a white man living in the 1800s.

Dr. Seaver gave his book the colorful title *A Narrative of the Life of Mrs. Mary Jemison, Who Was Taken by the Indians, in the Year 1755, When Only about Twelve Years of Age, and Has Continued to Reside amongst Them to the Present Time.* It became so popular that it sold more than 100,000 copies in 1824, the year it was published.

Other people added material to the book after Dr. Seaver's death. Some tried to show the American Indians as ignorant savages. One person even wrote a chapter about Mary's husband Hiokatoo, calling him an evil man. Others corrected misspellings and incorrect dates. For example, someone discovered that Mary was actually captured in 1758, not 1755.

Dr. Seaver did not seem to have asked Mary anything about her life as a Seneca woman taking part in tribal ceremonies or community life. Or maybe she was not willing to talk to him about such personal matters. Later editors added material to show that Mary, who was born a white Christian, rejected American Indian practices at the end of her life and returned to her Christian beliefs. For seventy-five years, however, she was a willing member of her tribe.

After a brief illness, Mary Jemison died in September 1833. She was ninety years old. She was given a Christian funeral and laid to rest in the burial ground of the Seneca Mission Church on the Buffalo Creek Reservation.

In 1859 a wealthy businessman named William Pryor Letchworth bought seven hundred acres of land on the Genesee River that was sacred to the Iroquois. Letchworth was interested in the American Indian peoples who had lived in that area. He was especially interested in Mary Jemison. He decided to set aside some of his land as a memorial to Mary and the Senecas. Letchworth moved a Seneca council house and the home of Mary Jemison's daughter Nancy to his land. Mary's remains were brought to the land and reburied there at the request of her family.

Letchworth's most visible tribute to Mary is the bronze statue made by the sculptor H. K. Bush-Brown in 1910. It stands in Letchworth State Park.

Mary Jemison's life bridged two worlds, the white settlers' and the American Indians'. She was brought to a frontier that was full of danger and promise. She grew into maturity with Native Americans who were being pushed off their lands and who were caught between European powers at war. She lived as a Seneca wife and mother through the French and Indian War, the American Revolution, and the War of 1812. She became a naturalized citizen of the United States in 1817, but she chose to remain with her American Indian friends and family.

Mary was more than just a survivor. She was the heroine of her own life story. "My strength has been great for a woman of my size," she said. "Otherwise I must long ago have died under the burdens which I was obliged to carry."

Timeline

1743   Mary Jemison is born at sea, on way from Ireland to America.

1758   She is captured by Shawnee Indians near Gettysburg, Pennsylvania.

1760   She marries Sheninjee, a Delaware Indian.

1762   Her first son, Thomas, is born.
Mary, Thomas, and her Seneca brothers travel from Ohio to Little Beard's Town in New York State. Sheninjee dies.

1765   Mary marries Hiokatoo, a Seneca Indian.

1779   Little Beard's Town is destroyed by American soldiers. Mary and her children take shelter on the Gardeau Flats, along the Genesee River.

1784   Mary is offered a chance to return to the white world. She decides to stay with the Senecas.

1797   She is given ownership of Gardeau Flats by the Iroquois council.

1811   Hiokatoo dies at age 103.

1817   Mary becomes a naturalized U.S. citizen.

1823   She tells her life story to Dr. James Seaver.

1831   She sells her land and moves to Buffalo Creek Reservation.

1833   Mary dies at age ninety.

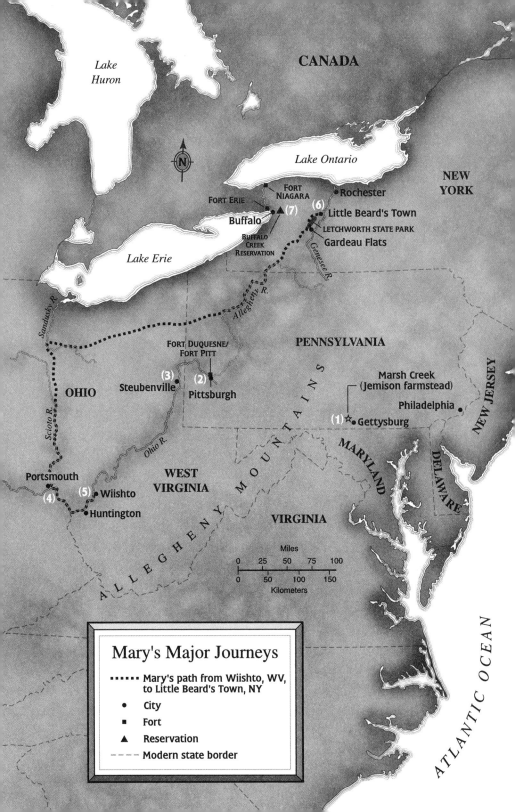

Lake Huron

CANADA

Lake Ontario

NEW YORK

N

FORT NIAGARA
FORT ERIE
▲ (7)
(6)
Buffalo
Rochester
Little Beard's Town
LETCHWORTH STATE PARK
Gardeau Flats
BUFFALO CREEK RESERVATION

Lake Erie

Sandusky R.

Allegheny R.

Genesee R.

PENNSYLVANIA

FORT DUQUESNE/ FORT PITT

OHIO

Steubenville
(3)
(2)
Pittsburgh

Marsh Creek (Jemison farmstead)

Philadelphia

(1) ☆ Gettysburg

NEW JERSEY

Scioto R.

Ohio R.

WEST VIRGINIA

MARYLAND

DELAWARE

Portsmouth
(4)
(5) ● Wiishto
● Huntington

VIRGINIA

A L L E G H E N Y   M O U N T A I N S

Miles
0   25   50   75   100
0   50   100   150
Kilometers

ATLANTIC OCEAN

Mary's Major Journeys

•••••• Mary's path from Wiishto, WV, to Little Beard's Town, NY
●   City
■   Fort
▲   Reservation
– – –   Modern state border

SITES MARKED ON MAP

(1) Mary's family lived near Gettysburg, Pennsylvania. This is where she was captured in 1758 by Shawnee Indians.

(2) At Fort Duquesne (later Fort Pitt) near Pittsburgh, Pennsylvania, Mary's captors gave her to two Seneca women.

(3) Mary was taken by canoe on the Ohio River to a Seneca town near Steubenville, Ohio.

(4) Mary's Seneca family spent winters near Portsmouth, Ohio.

(5) In Mary's second year with the Senecas, her tribe moved to Wiishto, on the Ohio River twenty miles from Huntington, West Virginia.

(6) In 1762 Mary traveled from Wiishto to her Seneca family's home on the Genesee River about thirty miles south of Rochester, New York. It took six months to travel nearly seven hundred miles.

(7) Mary died on the Buffalo Creek Reservation in 1833 at the age of ninety.

Bibliography

Kasson, Joy S. *Marble Queens and Captives: Women in Nineteenth-Century American Sculpture.* New Haven, CT: Yale University Press, 1990.

Namias, June. *White Captives: Gender and Ethnicity on the American Frontier.* Chapel Hill: University of North Carolina Press, 1993.

Nies, Judith. *Native American History: A Chronology of the Vast Achievements of a Culture and Their Links to World Events.* New York: Ballantine Books, 1996.

Seaver, James E. *The Life of Mary Jemison: The White Woman of the Genesee.* 5th ed. 1877. Edited by William Pryor Letchworth. Scituate, MA: Digital Scanning, Inc., 2001.

The quotations in this biography were taken from the Seaver book.

Further Reading

Aller, Susan Bivin. *Tecumseh.* Minneapolis: Lerner Publications Company, 2004. This book provides a brief history of the great Shawnee leader Tecumseh.

The Diary of Mary Jemison, Captured by Indians. Edited by Connie and Peter Roop. New York: Benchmark Books, 2001. The Roops select and edit excerpts from Dr. James Seaver's book to tell Mary's story to young readers.

Sherrow, Victoria. *The Iroquois Indians.* New York: Chelsea House, 1992. This book describes the culture and history of the Senecas and other Iroquois nations.

Yue, Charlotte, and David Yue. *The Wigwam and the Longhouse.* Boston: Houghton Mifflin, 2000. Illustrations and simple text introduce readers to the traditional lifestyles and dwellings of Eastern Woodland Indians, such as the Senecas.

Websites

Exploring Letchworth Park History
http://www.letchworthparkhistory.com
This site has information about Mary Jemison and links to photographs of her gravesite and statue in Letchworth State Park.

The Seneca Nation of Indians
http://www.sni.org
The official website of the Seneca of New York provides news, maps of reservations, and more.

Stories from PA History
http://www.explorepahistory.com/story.php
Visitors to this site can find historical background, maps, and photos about the French and Indian War in Pennsylvania.

The Sullivan-Clinton Campaign: History, the Iroquois, and George Washington
http://sullivanclinton.com
This site provides details of the attacks led by American generals John Sullivan and James Clinton on the Iroquois during the American Revolution.

Index

63

About the Author

Susan Bivin Aller is the author of biographies about Mark Twain, Louisa May Alcott, George Eastman, Ulysses S. Grant, and others. She is a former magazine editor and newspaper columnist. Aller is a member of the Advisory Council for the Connecticut Center for the Book and a judge for the Connecticut Book Awards. She collects antique children's books and lives with her two cats in Connecticut.

About the Illustrator

Laurie Harden is an illustrator and painter and has been, it seems, for all her life. It is her first love and all she has ever wanted to do. Harden studied at the Kansas City Art Institute and the Rhode Island School of Design (RISD). She graduated from RISD with a bachelor of fine arts in illustration. She continues to study independently. Her work is widely sought, exhibited, awarded, commissioned, and collected. An artist with an international clientele, Harden also teaches art privately. She resides in northern New Jersey.